Moments Along
a Journey of
Faith

To Jim:
God's Blessings
x
Keep the Faith.
— Don Threadle

MOMENTS ALONG
A JOURNEY OF
FAITH

D O N   T H R A S H E R

Providence House Publishers

PROVIDENCE PUBLISHING CORPORATION

FRANKLIN, TENNESSEE

Printed in the United States of America

06   05   04   03   02   1   2   3   4   5

Library of Congress Catalog Card Number: 2002108927

ISBN: 1-57736-274-8

Cover photos by Don Thrasher

Cover design by Gary Bozeman

The cover picture is the pier at Epworth By the Sea on St. Simons Island, Georgia.

The back cover picture is sunset at Saint Simons Island, Georgia.

Providence House Publishers
PROVIDENCE PUBLISHING CORPORATION
238 Seaboard Lane • Franklin, Tennessee 37067
800-321-5692
www.providencepubcorp.com

To the glory of God,
and in much appreciation
of my parents

WILLIAM HARWELL THRASHER SR.
August 25, 1917–November 12, 1983

and

HELEN FINGER THRASHER
November 15, 1920–

for their faith, unconditional love,
humor, and unyielding support.

CONTENTS

Errata

The publisher acknowledges the following editorial correction:

(1) On page ix, in the second paragraph, the third sentence should read:

One such leap earned him a brief spot on the dean's list at Georgia College.

(2) On page 2, in the first paragraph, the first sentence should read:

When I was a child, Mom and Dad used to drive us up to Gainesville, Georgia, so that we could spend Christmas Eve with Grandmama and Granddaddy Finger.

(3) On page 21, in the first paragraph, the first sentence should read:

In December 1975, I received my acceptance letter from the seminary at SMU.

FOREWORD

G od is always with us, and Don Thrasher's personal reflections remind us to recognize Him in our daily walk. Whether the subject is his family, his favorite place for spiritual nourishment, or a spilled pan of macaroni and cheese, the underlying message is that God loves us.

Like all of us, Don has faced challenges on his journey. But the reader will be struck by the tenacity of his faith and his realization that while true faith is a gift from God, it also requires a leap, an act of will on our part. One such leap earned him a brief spot on the dean's list at West Georgia College.

Those who are familiar with Georgia will recognize many of the names and places. Those who are not will learn something about the South and find universal themes of hope, humility, and the power of prayer. Each short passage concludes with the message Don learned from his experiences. They are messages we can all take to heart.

Russ Spencer
Alpharetta, Georgia

PREFACE

All of us have individual walks with God. We each have memorable moments in our faith journeys. As you read this book, I feel certain that there are some instances that you will relate to because you may have had similar experiences in your life. May God bless you!

HOLY GROUND

I love the Georgia coast! I love its beauty as well as its peacefulness. From Savannah on down, there's something special about that area. Savannah, especially, is really neat. Its history is amazing as well as all of the city's town squares. It literally took me two years to find John Wesley's statue there.

Near Savannah is Tybee Island. It is an ocean community and not a resort. I love its community feel. I also love its beautiful beach, which is a great place to walk. One November on a brief excursion there, I saw the sun rise over the beach. It was awesome.

I also enjoy St. Simons Island, which has now become more of a resort. What I love about this particular island is Epworth By the Sea, a United Methodist Retreat Center. Epworth's setting is among hanging moss trees along the Frederica River. The place is beautiful and extremely peaceful. It also has historical significance because John Wesley actually preached on its grounds.

My favorite spot at Epworth is its pier. It is one of the places where I can go to get away, reflect, and pray. I feel close to God there. To me, it is holy ground.

God provides places for us to go for rest and restoration.

THE PRINCE OF PEACE

When I was a child, Mom and Dad used to drive us up to Gainesville, Florida, so that we could spend Christmas Eve with Grandmama and Granddaddy Finger. My Aunt Martha and Uncle Haskell and their kids would join us as well as my aunts and uncles from out of state. We would all have a delicious turkey and dressing dinner that Grandmama would cook. Afterwards we would go into the living room and open presents. It would be a fun and festive day.

On Christmas Eve 1959, we drove from Decatur to Gainesville. The interstate, I-85, was completed only in Buford and Suwanee, so we had to drive the state roads to Gainesville. On that particular Christmas Eve, it was a rainy day. Also, there was much road construction because a bridge was being built on that highway. As a result, the roads were muddy. Guess whose car got stuck in the mud?

Our 1955 White Plymouth Savoy sedan was spinning mud up its back fenders. We knew that we were going to be late for dinner with Grandmama and Granddaddy. Dad got out and hitchhiked to Buford so we could have a wrecker pull us out of the mud. So, there we were—Mom and her five kids, ages two to nine, locked in a car awaiting help. We were scared but calm.

About thirty to forty minutes later, Dad came back with a wrecker which pulled us out of the mud. He had also called our family in Gainesville to let them know the situation. We made it to Gainesville and had a wonderful Christmas Eve.

Looking back over that experience some forty-two years ago, I can see God's hand in it.

We experienced "the Prince of Peace."

FAMILY VACATIONS

I can remember it just like it was yesterday. In August 1962, our family got ready to go on a family vacation to Ormond Beach, Florida. We would drive down there in the Thrasher station wagon and stay at the Elinor Village Cottages. Our vacation would last a week. We always had a good time going to the beach.

On this particular trip, Dad loaded our luggage carrier and placed it on top of our white 1958 Plymouth Belvedere station wagon (the one with the push-button automatic transmission). Mom would gather the picnic basket loaded with food for our growing family and place it in the car.

It was time for us to load the car. Dad then called us for the last time for pit stops. Everyone who needed one headed to the house for one last trip before we started. Dad then locked the house. We all got into the car. Dad started the engine. Mom started counting heads just to make sure that all of us were on board.

Suddenly, we heard some crying. It was my then five-year-old sister Mary. She was standing on our screened front porch just sobbing. She was in the house for one last pit stop. Mary thought that we were going to leave without her. She didn't want to be forgotten. Mom went in and hugged her, took her to the car, and we proceeded with our vacation.

Jesus didn't forget us on the cross.

HELPING OUT

I grew up in a very traditional household. With five children to raise, my mother worked as a professional homemaker while my father worked as a hospital administrator.

As a boy, I would always walk into the kitchen before supper time. Mom was always in there doing her cooking and preparations. I would ask her, "Mom, what's for supper?" She would smile and tell me the menu. Then I would go back outside or to my room to play.

At times, I would go into the kitchen and ask her, "Mom, is there anything that I can do to help?" Her eyes would instantly light up. Sometimes she needed help. I would help set the table, put the ice in the glasses, and pour the tea or lemonade.

Other times she didn't need help. However, she would always appreciate it when any of us, my brothers and sisters included, offered. I could tell by her reaction.

Even though we don't intentionally mean to, we all at different times take our families, friends, and even our church for granted. But when we offer someone help, their faces often light up in appreciation. These people always feel better because they didn't have to ask for it.

Let's show our love for God by helping others out.
There are plenty of opportunities.

5

THAT TRIP TO THE VARSITY

I remember my first trip to the Varsity restaurant. It was when I was about seven years old. We all got into the Thrasher family station wagon and drove to downtown Atlanta. Dad told us about the Varsity as we went there. He told us a little bit about its history and even about people who ate there. He also told us about some of its famous staff members.

When we drove in, he and Mom felt that it would be better for our brood of five kids to eat in the car and experience curb service. (Little did I know then that fifteen years later I would actually have a summer stint myself as a curb waiter at Steak 'n Shake.) The curb waiter from the Varsity came out to our Plymouth wagon and took our order.

One can imagine the waiter trying to take an order from five different kids. Whenever my family drove into McDonald's, the staff there always would press the panic button.

Dad decided that he would order "dressed hamburgers" for all of us. When our order arrived, we thought that dressed meant having mustard, ketchup, and pickle on the burger. Instead, it had the works which also included lettuce, tomato, and mayonnaise. I can still remember him throwing his hands in the air and then him and Mom scraping off the topping of each hamburger because their kids didn't want dressed burgers.

God's grace was shown that night.

THE FRONT PORCH

My maternal grandparents lived in Gainesville, Georgia. They had an older home on Ridgewood Avenue. Its small floor plan consisted of two bedrooms, one bathroom, a living room, a dining room, a kitchen, and an enclosed back porch. There was a small white picket fence that surrounded the front yard.

The house also had a fairly big front porch. Because my grandparents did not have air conditioning in their home, we would sit out on the front porch during our visits on hot afternoons. It was the coolest place.

Out on the porch, we would sit in one of several rocking chairs or on the porch swing. We would then talk or play games or listen to my grandfather's stories. We always had good visits. Many other times we would just sit back and watch the cars drive by. I can still hear the sound of the cars traveling on their cement street. It was like we were being spectators on life. We were just sitting and watching.

Without knowing it, we can also be spectators at the church. Sometimes, it's very comfortable to sit back and watch things happen. At times, we need to do this. At other times, we need to do our part.

Let's show our love for God and for His church by getting off the porch and becoming involved.

JUMPLIGHTS

Do you know what a jumplight is? I have found that many people do not know what I am talking about. They have never heard of it. I grew up with the term. It is quite common in Decatur and east Georgia. Perhaps it is more common in the Thrasher household. Maybe my dad made up the name.

A jumplight is not a traffic light that jumps up and down. Instead, it is a traffic light with an arrow that lets traffic turn left first in heavily congested intersections. With it, one gets a jump ahead of the other drivers.

Jumplights are all around. You can see them everywhere. Most major streets and roadways have them. Now, even smaller streets have them. I have heard of other names for a jumplight. Some call it the "arrow" while others call it the "advanced turning signal." Whatever we call it, we mean the same thing.

There are many different denominations in our world. We may differ with our names, beliefs, and doctrines. Despite those differences, we all have a common bond.

Jesus Christ is our Lord and Savior.

CAR COLLECTIONS

I love cars. I have ever since I was a child. I used to collect car brochures to increase my knowledge about different models. Currently, I have a collection of model cars. In my office, I have a model of the new Volkswagen Beetle as well as a model (and radio) of the 1955 Chevrolet Corvette. Recently, I bought a model of the 2001 Chrysler PT Cruiser as well as a model of the 2002 Ford Thunderbird.

I remember when the Ford Taurus/Mercury Sable models came out in 1985. At that time, I thought those cars were ugly. I predicted that they would not sell. Well, I was wrong. Those models became best-sellers and are still going strong today. The main reason these cars have been so successful is what is on the inside rather than simply how they look. Over the years, I have gotten used to their looks. (I am also trying to get used to the looks of the Chrysler PT Cruiser.) Now I think they are beautiful creations.

How do we look at people? Do we look only at the outside instead of the inside? Do we give them a fair chance? Do we look at them through the eyes of God? If we do, we can find that they are beautiful creations in His image.

We all are beautiful creations in God's eyes.

9

My First Date

In December 1968, I went on my very first date. It was a double date with my older sister and her boyfriend. I took his sister out. We were all planning to see a double feature at the Fox Theatre in Atlanta, Georgia. The movies were Walt Disney's *The Horse in the Grey Flannel Suit* and *Winnie the Pooh*. Afterwards, we were planning to go to the Varsity or Krispy Kreme for refreshments.

I was fourteen years old. Since it was my official first date, I was also excited but nervous. I shaved for the first time that night even though my beard consisted only of peach fuzz. After my shave, I poured on half a bottle of English Leather cologne. I wanted to look and smell good.

The date went fine. After the movie, I was walking back to the car with her. As we were walking, I told my date to watch out for a missing step that I noticed in the parking lot. She did. I didn't. Guess who fell? I was unhurt but embarrassed. I think that it started a trend in my life. Many times when I get excited or nervous about something, I turn into a klutz.

Years later, a prominent female Atlanta news anchor was the Fifth Sunday speaker when I was on staff at Harmony Grove United Methodist Church in Lilburn. After introducing her, I was so excited about her visit that I wasn't watching where I was going. Guess who fell off the stage? It wasn't the news anchor.

When we fall in life, God gives us a hand to help us back up.

10

STUDY HALL

When I was a freshman at Decatur High School, I signed up to take a study hall for one period to help with schoolwork. Study hall is a non-credit class period which students utilize for studying, catching up on some sleep, or for reading. There is no talking during study hall. My study hall period was during the fifth period, from 1:00–2:00, after lunch and before my French 1 class. There were times when I did some homework. However, there were many more times when I just sat there quietly. I thought it was boring.

One day a friend of mine had a sneezing fit during study hall. It was an allergic reaction to pollen. He sneezed thirty-five times in a row. I was so bored that I counted his sneezes.

That episode was a turning point for me. For the next academic year and the ones that followed until I graduated, I decided not to add study hall to my class schedule. Instead, I chose to take one more class each year. My schedule was heavy but well balanced. I was never bored again in a high school class.

I can remember another turning point for me. It was while I was in college. I was majoring in management and very unhappy (and even bored) with my course work. I was also fighting my call into professional ministry. My life changed that summer because I finally accepted my call into the ministry, changed my major to psychology/pre-theology, and felt God's peace. The rest is history. Turning points can and do happen at different times in our lives.

Through changes in our lives, God can get our attention and turn our lives around.

My College Acceptance

In December 1971, I received my acceptance to Georgia College (GC) in Milledgeville. I was a senior at Decatur High School at the time. I was happy to receive the acceptance and made plans to attend college there the following fall quarter.

I knew that God was leading me to Georgia College, but I didn't know why at the time. However, I did not want to tell my fellow classmates at Decatur where I was going to college. In fact, I kept it quiet for five whole months until it was announced in the senior plans section in our school newspaper *The Scribbler*. Before that, I would change the subject if someone asked me what my college plans were.

My reason is that I didn't want to be kidded by my friends about the town where my college was located. I knew they would say that Milledgeville was a good match for me or that I would fit right in in Milledgeville. You see, the town is the home of the state mental hospital. I didn't want to be kidded for five months. I was too self-conscious.

In late May 1972, the word got out about my college plans. There was some kidding; however, it was not as much as I expected. Instead, most everyone was very excited and supportive of my college choice.

When I moved down to Milledgeville the following fall, I found out that the state mental hospital wasn't located there. Instead, it was located in Hardwick outside of the town. Through my studies at GC, I actually did a tour of the hospital and did an independent study there. It's a fascinating and interesting place.

Are we too self-conscious to talk about our Christian faith?

12

LEAVING FOR COLLEGE

It was Sunday, September 17, 1972. It was the day that I moved into my dorm room at Georgia College in Milledgeville. I was about to begin my freshman year in college.

We left Decatur early that morning in our 1970 Oldsmobile Vista Cruiser filled with Dad, Mom, Doug, and me. That station wagon was fully loaded with both my things as well as my brother's.

Our parents decided to take us to college in one trip. They would drop me off at my college in Milledgeville and then take Doug on down to his college at Valdosta State. (He transferred the very next quarter to the University of Georgia.)

After my belongings were unloaded to my dorm room and I said my farewells to my folks, I walked into Napier Hall. I was about to begin a whole new chapter of my life called college. My dorm was brand new and I was actually the first resident to move into it that fall.

I began to unpack my belongings. New residents started to move into the dorm and I said my hellos. It took me over an hour to make my bed from scratch that day. I know that it was because I was anxious and nervous.

Later that afternoon, I walked next door to the Wesley Foundation House where there were welcoming arms and delicious refreshments. The Wesley Foundation is the United Methodist campus ministry. From my very first day on campus to the day that I graduated, I was an active member of Wesley. They were my church family during my college years.

It does not matter what stage of life that we are in.
God provides us a family of faith through the church.

13

GRUB DAY

When I was a student there, Georgia College was known as a suitcase college. Many students stayed at the college during the week but went home on the weekends. Some went home every weekend. The ones that did felt that there was nothing to do in Milledgeville on the weekends. Georgia College didn't have a football team but it had other activities. In addition, Milledgeville is a very historic town. There is a lot to see.

I went home to Decatur for the weekend about once a month. On the weekends that I stayed on campus, I would usually spend time with friends, participate in some college activities such as the Wesley Foundation, catch up on some studying, and do some walking around town.

On Saturdays, I would have "grub day." I wouldn't shave that day (in my early college days, I didn't need to shave every day due to peach fuzz!), and I would wear old clothes. I felt grubby which also felt pretty good.

On Sunday morning, my grub day would end. I would shower and shave and get ready for church. I would then go to worship at either the Wesley Foundation at GC or at the First United Methodist Church of Milledgeville. Afterwards, I felt good because I felt cleansed. It got me going for the week.

These days, it is rare that I have a grub day. However, I do have a grub morning. I shower and shave after I have my daily quiet time with God. Afterwards, I feel spiritually and physically cleansed. It gets me going for the day.

Prayer and worship are means for us to be cleansed by God.

14

MAKING CHANGES

When I was a sophomore at Georgia College, I went through a period of unhappiness and uneasiness. I was somewhat bored with my classes, fighting a call to go into professional ministry, and getting tired of life in Milledgeville. I was going through and dealing with the sophomore blahs.

Thoughts of transferring to another college came to mind. Of course, the grass is always greener somewhere else. In fact, I even received catalogs from other schools. I did not want to tough it out. I wanted to give up and go someplace different. However, a nudge from God kept me there. With time, however, I found that I needed to make a change.

That change was within me. First, I needed to change my attitude from negative to positive. Second, I needed to change my career focus from business to ministry. Third, I needed to change my major from business management to psychology/pre-theology.

With God's help, I did all three. As a result, my last two years at Georgia College were full of happy blessings. In fact, they were the best years of my college days.

We all face tough times. It doesn't matter where we are in life. It is a fact that tough times will come and they will also go. When they arrive, we as Christians and as a church cannot be afraid to tough those times out. With this, God calls us to make a change within our attitudes, our focus, and ourselves.

If we make changes, who knows
what blessings we could receive.

15

ROOM 208A

Room 208A of Napier Hall was where I lived during my sophomore year at Georgia College. That room brings back a treasure chest full of memories. During that year, I decided to major in business management and wanted to work as a manager at Walt Disney World. At the same time, I was active in the Wesley Foundation and fighting my call into the professional ministry.

It was a rocky school year. The business courses were difficult. I even flunked an economics course after spending an entire quarter trying to understand it. I was unhappy and felt out of place in the business department. Toward the end of the spring quarter, I felt the need to go to summer school to make up that economics course. I did go that summer but the direction of my life changed.

After wrestling with God all year, I got down on my knees in room 208A in early July 1974 and I accepted my call into the professional ministry. I also changed my major to psychology/pre-theology. As a result, I became more motivated and excited. My grades went up. I felt God's peace. I became a new and different Don.

Years later, a young man from a church that I was serving visited Georgia College with me. We walked around campus. We then walked into Napier Hall. As we approached room 208A, I shared with him my story about that room and how my life was changed.

A few minutes later, the current resident of room 208A walked out into the hall. We met and I asked him his major. He said, "I believe that God is calling me into the ministry."

We may be surprised where God calls us.

THE TRAVEL SCHOLARSHIP

In March 1975 while a student at Georgia College, I felt led by God to explore the ministries in the Hollywood, California, area. I did not know if God wanted me to serve there in ministry or if He wanted to show me something. I just felt an urge to see the place.

To my surprise, two months later I received a Christian travel scholarship from an honor society that I was inducted into. The travel scholarship could be used to explore ministries anywhere in the world. I decided to use the scholarship to explore ministries in Hawaii and in California.

Before I made my trip, I wrote to the Los Angeles district superintendent to find out if there was a First United Methodist Church of Hollywood. I also gave him the name of the hotel where I was staying in Hollywood.

A few weeks later, I received a letter from the district superintendent in Los Angeles. He told me that there was indeed a First UMC of Hollywood and that the church was located directly across the street from the hotel where I was staying. I believe that God wanted me to visit that church.

In August 1975, I made my trip out there. I had the opportunity to visit with one of the staff ministers of that church. He told me about the ins and outs of Hollywood life and their ministries to the community. I left feeling that God wanted me to serve out there.

I was wrong. In the years since that visit and a second visit to northern California, I found that the doors were closed for me to do ministry there. For some of us, God calls us to serve in faraway places. That's not the case for most of us.

God wants each of us to serve right where we are.

HOUSEPLANTS

When I was in college, my mother gave me a spider plant for my dorm room. This was my first experience of taking care of a houseplant. My mother has a green thumb in this area. I don't. For a while, the plant was doing okay with my weekly watering. In the middle of the quarter, I noticed that it started to get white spots on it. I thought that the plant was sick so I threw it away.

I told my mother about the plant and what I did with it. Her response shocked me. She told me that my plant was okay and the white spots were part of its leaves. I sure misread that plant.

When I lived in a parsonage in Powder Springs, Georgia, there was an empty flower pot on my deck. So, I decided to pour in a bag of sunflower seeds. That flower pot was full to its brim. I did not do a thing with it. In fact, the rain watered it. To my astonishment, the sunflowers bloomed beautifully.

It's interesting. Those experiences with the plants taught me something—we can give up on our faith, be lazy about taking care of it, or we can become active participants in our faith.

Thank God that He doesn't give up on us!

18

"OLD SALLY"

When I was in college, my dad bought a used car to help us with our transportation needs. It was a 1962 Mercury Comet four-door sedan. He bought the ten-year-old car for one dollar from my great uncle. We named it "Old Sally" and took turns taking it to college.

During my senior year of college, I drove that car. I learned that it had its own personality. If I floored it, the car went thirty-five miles per hour. If I rolled down the back window on the right door, the window would fall into the door. The car had the vacuum-type windshield wipers. If you put your foot on the gas pedal, the wipers would slow down. If you took your foot off the gas pedal, they would speed up. That's great for a rainstorm on the expressway!

One Friday evening, I took some friends to the Milledgeville mall. At that time, my car horn wouldn't work. I got mad and said, "This stupid horn never works!" As soon as I made that statement, the horn got stuck. I hit the side of the steering wheel to stop it.

From then on, every time I made a right turn, the car's horn would honk. When that happened, the only polite thing that I could do is to wave at folks. With its horn problem, the car could easily be found if it was stolen. We had that car in the family for four more years. My twin brother sold it for fifty dollars to buy a car seat when his daughter was born.

Cars come and go, but God's love for each of us is constant.

Winning a Trip

In May 1975, I won a trip to Hawaii and California. The trip was planned for ten days that August and would include stays on the islands of Oahu, Kauai, and Maui as well as a trip to Hollywood, California, and Disneyland. The trip was arranged through a travel agency and a friend from my church planned to go with me.

On August 21, 1975, we flew from Atlanta to Los Angeles and then took a connecting flight to Honolulu. Both flights were good. On the American Express flyer, it said that we would have a flower lei greeting at the airport upon arrival. I pictured a beautiful hula dancer greeting us.

When we arrived, there was indeed a flower lei greeting. However, there was no hula dancer in sight. Instead, a big fella (he looked more like a wrestler) found us and threw the flower leis at us. We were disappointed, but we got over it. I guess that we expected too much.

Our biggest surprise came from a resident of Honolulu. Her mother belonged to the church that I was serving that summer in Carrollton, Georgia. In fact, her mother had lived with her in Hawaii and had recently died. She had flown to Atlanta earlier that August with her mother's ashes for burial in the Carrollton Church cemetery.

While in Carrollton, she invited us to call her when we got to Honolulu. We did and she took us out to lunch overlooking the most beautiful ocean bluffs of Oahu. I will never forget her Christian hospitality. What a blessing. It made that trip.

Human expectations can lead to disappointment. Turning our expectations over to God can lead to many blessings.

20

WAITING ON GOD

H ave you ever waited on God for something? I can well remember one of my first experiences on waiting. In fact, I will never forget it. In June 1975, I was a senior at Georgia College. I felt led by God to go into professional ministry and into seminary. During that month, I applied for admission to seminary at Southern Methodist University (SMU).

The application was made on faith and I waited for an answer. A month went by and I didn't hear anything except the acknowledgement that they received my application. Two months and still no word. The fall quarter came upon us. I grew anxious but still no word. Those fall months went by slowly. The thought of not knowing was uneasy for me.

Finally, on December 22, 1975, I received the official letter from SMU. It was their letter informing me of my acceptance into seminary there. I was overjoyed after a long six-month wait. However, it was a wonderful Christmas present that year.

Waiting is hard. When we wait, we need to take care of ourselves emotionally, physically, and spiritually. We also need to focus on and trust in God. If we do and also do our part, we can then sit back and watch God work.

Waiting is a matter of faith and of trust.

21

An Academic Miracle

I n December 1975, I received my acceptance letter from the seminary school at SMU. The following quarter was my final one at Georgia College. I was scheduled to complete my courses for my degree in March. Graduation was scheduled for June.

In order to maintain my seminary acceptance, I had to have a minimum overall grade point average from college. The fall quarter of 1975 was a hard one. My grades consisted of a B, C, and a D. My overall grade point average was below the one I needed to maintain for seminary.

I got out my calculator to find out what grades I needed to make for my final quarter to keep my seminary acceptance. To my shock, I had to make straight As. I couldn't believe it because I had never made straight As in my entire life. Academics did not come easy to me.

I prayed, "Lord, if you want me to go to seminary, please give me the strength and the wisdom to make those grades." I took a leap of faith, set a goal, and went to work.

My course load was pretty heavy. I took two senior-level psychology courses (including an independent study), a New Testament introduction course, and I rejoined the college choir. I had to really buckle down. I also did a lot of praying. At the end of the quarter, I received my grades. I made straight As and even made the dean's list. It was an academic miracle with the help of God, much prayer, and hard work. The rest is history.

Have you taken a leap of faith lately?

22

CHOIR TOUR

In August 1976, right before I started seminary, I went with a group of youth and young adults from my home church (Decatur First UMC) on a week-long choir tour to Tennessee, Kentucky, Ohio, and West Virginia. Our tour group was called the Summer Players. We presented a musical comedy program with a deep spiritual message to several churches along our tour. My youngest sister, Mary, was part of our touring group.

Besides the programs, we also did some sightseeing. The whole area was scenic and was filled with beautiful hills and valleys. We went to the Opryland Park, a Kentucky horse farm, and drove through the countryside of eastern Ohio. When we got to the West Virginia state line, we all sang John Denver's "Country Roads." During our visit to West Virginia, we visited a glass factory.

At that glass factory, Mary and I spotted a beautiful royal blue cut-glass water pitcher. We decided to chip in together and buy that pitcher as a gift for Mom. We thought that she could use it for water, lemonade, or iced tea. After we got home from the tour, we presented her with our gift. She was thrilled beyond words. She thought the pitcher was beautiful.

However, until this day some twenty-five years later, she does not utilize the pitcher for water, lemonade, or iced tea. Instead, she has placed it in a special spot in the house and has used it for a flower vase. There are times that she does not place anything in it because she believes that the pitcher is beautiful by itself. She treasures it.

Do we treasure our Christian faith?

23

THE SMU POSTER

When I was in the eighth grade, I wanted to attend Southern Methodist University when it was time for me to go to college. I wanted to go where all the Methodists went! In fact, I even had a poster of the SMU campus on my room's bulletin board.

A few years later, my dream of going to SMU changed when our parents told the rest of us that we could attend any state college or university of our choice within the university system of Georgia. My older brother Harwell was attending Massachusetts Institute of Technology (MIT) on scholarship. With five kids to put through school, we understood. That is why I chose to go to Georgia College in Milledgeville.

On the whole, my years at GC were wonderful! During my years there, I developed leadership skills through the Wesley Foundation and other campus activities. My faith grew and it was at GC where I accepted my call into the ministry.

Before my graduation from GC, I felt led to go to seminary. I wanted to go where God wanted me to go. After researching several United Methodist seminaries, I came to the conclusion that God was leading me to the Perkins School of Theology at SMU in Dallas, Texas. I applied, was accepted, and received a partial scholarship there.

In the fall of 1976, after my college graduation, I enrolled at Perkins. Within a week, I received a letter from my dad. He said, "We were going through a closet the other day and we found the old SMU poster. Dreams do come true, son."

I originally wanted to go to SMU for college. However, God had other plans. I got to go, but for seminary. Since then, I learned it wasn't just my dream.

It was God's dream, too.

24

TEXAS SNOWSTORMS

Texas is known for its weird weather. In early November 1976, during my first semester in seminary at Perkins, I can remember one day being sunny and seventy degrees. The very next morning was thirty-three degrees with three inches of snow on the ground.

During the winter of 1978, we had six snowfalls in six weeks. It was beautiful at first. However, it got old after a while. Schools were not closed and life went on. Driving around Dallas was truly an adventure during that time. The roads were damaged due to heavy ice and snow. As a result, there were many potholes in the road. One had to be really careful because a car's tires and chassis can be damaged by those potholes.

I can remember driving my 1972 Plymouth Gold Duster to and from the church that I was serving on staff at the time. The car slid at some places. I remember praying to God to help me get back to my apartment. He did.

Life can be full of storms. At times, we can be blanketed by those storms. At other times, there could be some damage that would leave potholes in our lives. When those storms arrive and leave some damage, we have a choice. We can panic and let it get to us, or we can trust God to see us through them.

God will pave the way!

ABSENTMINDED FOLKS

D uring my first year of seminary at SMU, I became friends with a fellow student who was at times absentminded. While in school, I worked part-time at the seminary library. About 4:30 P.M. one day when I was working, my friend Glenn came into the library and asked me when I was planning to go to supper at the SMU cafeteria. I got off work that day at 5:00 P.M. and I asked him to meet me at my dorm room then. He said that was fine and went back to the dorm.

At 4:40 P.M., he went to my room and knocked on the door. My roommate answered. Glenn said, "Is Don there?" My roommate told him that I didn't get off work until 5:00 P.M. Glenn said, "Oh yeah!" Glenn did that many times to many people. We laughed a lot about it. However, his absentmindedness got in the way of his academic work. He later dropped out of seminary.

Unfortunately, there are many people who are absentminded about the church. It is shown through their lack of attendance, service, and other ways of stewardship. Eventually, they drop out of the church.

What can we do? We can show them God's presence by reaching out, loving them, accepting them as they are, and welcoming them back.

Our absentminded folks may become presentminded folks.

SERVING COMMUNION

At age twenty-two, I assisted in a Holy Communion service for the first time in my life. It was during my first year of seminary at SMU in Dallas, Texas. I was asked by the Chapel Service Worship Committee to help serve Communion at one of our Tuesday chapel services.

I was excited and honored. I was also nervous. At the service, we served Communion by intinction or by dipping the bread into the cup. I wanted to make sure that I didn't drop the bread or the cup. The day came for that chapel service. After the sermon, the elder gave the signal for us to help serve the Communion.

The elder gave me the cup after serving me Communion. Somehow, I went off in the wrong direction, ran smack into the elder, and spilled half of the cup. No one was hurt but I sure was embarrassed. There was enough grape juice left in the cup, so I was able to serve all of the folks who came down to the Communion rail. They did not hold it against me for the accidental spill. In fact, I helped serve Communion several more times and didn't drop or spill anything.

Since then, I have assisted in Communion services in many churches and several times at annual conference. It is a special feeling serving Communion to your church family. It is also a special feeling receiving Communion with your church family. However, I will never forget the first time I helped serve Communion and what I learned from that experience.

Communion shows God's grace.

THE SURPRISE

During my first year of seminary, I corresponded with a female friend named Cathy from Georgia College. She was a senior and kept me up-to-date on what was going on at the college.

In September of that year, I wrote Cathy that I had a big surprise for her and my other friends. She wrote me back immediately and asked me what the surprise was. I wrote her and told her that the surprise would really shock folks. She again wrote me back and asked what the surprise was.

This type of correspondence kept going for two months. Finally, I wrote her that I was planning to come to visit the GC campus during my winter break but that wasn't the surprise.

She wrote me back and said, "I can't stand it any more! What's the surprise?" I wrote her back that I couldn't tell her or the others until January. She wasn't a happy camper but she was a good sport about it. She knew that my surprise would not be revealed until my visit.

In January, I made a trip to Milledgeville. When I got on campus, I ran into Cathy at the dining hall. My surprise was revealed. I grew a mustache during my first semester at seminary. Okay, it looked more like a hairlip. Cathy saw the mustache and asked, "Is that the surprise?" What a reaction. Life is full of surprises. At times, we anticipate too much. As a result, we are let down and disappointed.

God does not want us to anticipate, just to trust Him.

THE MACARONI EXPERIENCE

During my seminary days at Southern Methodist University in Dallas, Texas, I moved into my first apartment. It was a small white cottage behind a duplex that was a few blocks from campus. I shared the cottage with some guys from school.

One night, I had the opportunity to cook supper. It was my very first time cooking. I wanted to make sure that I did things right. I decided to make macaroni and cheese. I boiled the water and poured the package of macaroni into the pan. When it boiled, I turned down the burner. I then added the cheese sauce and the milk. I thought that it would be ready. However, it didn't look right. "Isn't it supposed to look thicker?" I asked myself. "What's not right?"

I finally read the directions. I then looked at the pan. I forgot to drain the macaroni! I had macaroni and cheese soup! In my haste to pour out the soup, I spilled the macaroni and cheese all over the white kitchen. It was a mess to clean up. I learned a powerful lesson that night. In life, one needs to read the directions.

Christian education helps direct people on how to lead a Christian life. It helps us answer the question "What next?" or "How can I grow?" in our individual walks with Christ.

Christian education helps us read the directions spiritually.

GRADES

A cademics were always difficult for me. I wonder if it was inherited. My dad had similar struggles. In fact, when he was a student at Emory University, he liked English 101 so much that he took it twice. I didn't have that struggle, but I had to work hard to maintain a B-minus overall grade point average. Some courses were harder for me. I usually made As and Bs in the elective or major courses.

In high school, I had about a 2.5 overall grade point average. I had the same overall grade point average in college as well as in seminary. The only place that I had an overall 4.0 grade point average was when I took that one postgraduate course at West Georgia College.

At graduation, there are some folks who graduate summa cum laude (with highest honor); there are some others that graduate magna cum laude (with high honor); and there are those who graduate cum laude (with honor). Then there are others like me that graduate praise the laude (with praise and thanksgiving to God for the opportunity to graduate). For the ones who don't graduate, they yell "Oh Laude!" (which means they need help).

I encourage each of us to do our best with the abilities and gifts that God has given each of us. That's all that we can do.

I wonder if God grades us.

THREE BIG EVENTS

As the congregation was singing "God of Grace and God of Glory," my twin brother, Doug, and I were recessing up the aisle with the other ordinands at Glenn Memorial United Methodist Church in Atlanta, Georgia. It was Wednesday, June 15, 1977. We were just ordained deacons and probationary members of the North Georgia Conference.

While walking up the aisle, we saw our parents. I will never forget their look. Our dad was beaming. Our mother, with her eyes filled with tears, walked into the aisle from their pew and embraced us both. It was a special night for our family. Our individual calls into the professional ministry were affirmed.

As the years went on since that night, our ministry journeys went different paths. Doug went on to get his elder's orders and pursued the pastoral ministry. He is now the senior pastor of Tuckston United Methodist Church in Athens, Georgia.

After years of struggling, I left the pastoral ministry in 1984 and felt God calling me into the Christian education ministry and to the diaconate. On June 18, 1987, I was consecrated a diaconal minister at the North Georgia Annual Conference. In 1996, the general conference of the United Methodist Church decided to ordain diaconals into full clergy. On June 11, 1997, almost twenty years after my first ordination, I was ordained a deacon in full connection at the North Georgia Conference. Life goes full circle at times.

Through our struggles, we do experience God's grace
as well as God's glory.

31

SOUND EFFECTS

A seminary friend of mine told me the following story while we were traveling on the 1980 seminary singers bus tour. The story was so funny that tears were streaming from my eyes, and I almost fell out of my bus seat. It also actually happened. Here it goes.

It was the first Sunday after this woman started college. She wanted to attend worship that morning at her college church. However, she was running late due to the fact that she overslept. She also skipped breakfast that morning. She did make it to worship and found a seat in a pew in the middle of the sanctuary. The worship service was very meaningful. The pastor got up to preach.

During his sermon, the pastor exclaimed, "Let us hunger for the Lord!" As soon as he preached that statement, the woman's stomach growled loudly. In fact, everyone in the sanctuary heard it. She wanted to crawl under a pew.

However, the pastor did not hear it. He kept on preaching. Minutes later, he exclaimed, "Let us have an appetite for the Holy Spirit!" Right on cue, the woman's stomach growled again even louder. The whole congregation started to quietly laugh. She was embarrassed, but her growling stomach taught her not to skip breakfast on Sunday morning. However, it did enhance that sermon.

God uses many ways (including sound effects)
to get our attention.

32

NICKNAMES

When my nephew Philip was beginning to talk, I asked him what his name was. He knew it because I had heard him say it before. I asked him again and he would not answer. So, I told him, "I'm going to call you Oscar!" Immediately, he screamed, "Oscar!" From then on, I gave him that nickname.

My oldest niece, Brianne, was some twenty months older and was talking well. When she heard that Philip had a nickname, she asked for one from me too. I asked her, "What do you want to be called?" She announced, "Bonkers!" So she received that nickname.

My oldest nephew, Christopher, heard about the nicknames. He was a little older than Philip and younger than Brianne. He asked for a nickname. I asked him, "What name do you want to be called?" He told me that he wanted to be called "Kelly." So, he received his nickname.

When my youngest nephew, Jordan, began to talk, I asked him what he wanted to be called. He said, "Eat Soup." So, I gave him that nickname.

For years, I called my niece "Bonkers" and nephews "Oscar," "Kelly," and "Eat Soup." We all had fun with those names throughout their childhoods, and it helped us to bond.

When they got older, I went back to calling them by their given names. However, they still remember their special nicknames that represent love and affection.

"Lord" is a wonderful nickname for Jesus.

THE POSTGRADUATE COURSE

West Georgia College (now the State University of West Georgia) in Carrollton is the only college or university in the nation that I had a 4.0 overall grade point average. Of course, I took only one class there.

It was in the fall of 1982. I was pastoring a small United Methodist church in Carroll County. At age twenty-eight, I was confused about the direction in which God was calling me in my life. I knew that it was going to be in the ministry but unsure about the pastorate.

West Georgia College was nearby. I looked at their graduate school catalog. Their school of education offered a master's degree in guidance and counseling. I decided to take an introductory course as a non-degree postgraduate student to help give me a sense of direction.

Little did I know then how that course began a journey of transition for my ministry and me. By the end of that course, I had decided to leave the local church pastoral ministry and head into a new direction of ministry.

I left Carroll County with mixed emotions. I did not know what God wanted me to do with my ministry, but I had to lean on God to show me the way. Within His time through ministry career guidance tests and through experiences, God showed me what He wanted me to do in ministry. It was and still is the ministry of Christian education.

Mary and Joseph had to lean on God as they prepared for the birth of Jesus. Their journey to Bethlehem was a trying but an incredible one. They showed us that we all have to hope and trust in God.

If we lean on God, He will show us the way.

34

THE NIGHT MY DAD DIED

At 2:15 A.M. on Saturday, November 12, 1983, I awoke to my mother screaming my name from upstairs. I got out of bed and ran up to Mom and Dad's room. There, I saw my dad's lifeless body. He had just died after a long battle with cancer. I looked at my grief-stricken mom. I told her, "He's gone." She fell into my arms. We held each other tight.

A little while later, Mom left the room to get ready because an ambulance was summoned to take Dad to the hospital. In my grief, I looked again at his body. I felt God's comfort.

When the ambulance reached the hospital, we entered the emergency room. Dad's body had to be pronounced dead by a physician for it to be given to Emory University. While waiting on the doctor, a couple came into the emergency room. She was ready to deliver her baby. Again, I felt God's comfort.

At 6:00 A.M. that morning, we were back at home beginning the process of funeral arrangements and facing our loss. I looked out the window. There, I saw the most vibrant sunrise in my entire life. My dad met God and became a citizen of heaven. I felt God's comfort. I still do today.

God's comfort can be shown in many ways.

35

MAD AT GOD?

Have you ever been mad at God? Wait a minute—what am I asking? We are never supposed to be mad at God. I am sure that all of us have experienced this sometime in our lives. I have.

The year was 1983. I will never forget it. Within the course of that year, I had left the pastorate, broken up with my fiancée, and watched my dad die of cancer. By the end of that year, I was empty and angry. I was going through several different grief processes all at the same time. My faith was struggling.

I was mad at God for a while. However, I still went though the motions of going to church. During my recovery, I did much reading. Through it, I learned a lot about life, myself, and God.

Many of us equate life with God. When we experience bad things in life, we blame God. We don't want to face the fact that life is hard at times. When we face this fact, we will see a different side of God. God is the one who comforts us and carries us through the hard times of life.

In the years since 1983, my Christian faith has changed and grown. I used to think that God had abandoned me when I experienced hard times. Now, I see Him holding and carrying me through them.

He will hold and carry all of us through difficult situations.

MY DOG, MYFFIE

I got her when she was nine weeks old. In June 1981, the youth group at Snellville United Methodist Church gave me a blond and apricot dachshund-poodle mix puppy as a going away present. I named her Myffie (short for the **M**ethodist **Y**outh **F**oundation) in honor of that youth group. (I could have named her Snellie but that name did not seem to fit her.)

Myffie was my first dog. In my childhood and youth, I had fish and a parakeet. My folks said adding a dog to the household of five kids would be a bit too much. I understood and hoped to get one when I was an adult. That dream finally came true on the night that I received her. As a puppy, Myffie looked like a dachshund with a perm. However, she grew up to be a beautiful doodle dog.

Myffie was a wonderful companion over the years. She and I used to go on long walks together. I even taught her a few tricks. For a single guy, she provided great company. She was one of my stabilizing forces during times of instability and stress. She was with me during my dad's illness and death. She was also with me during several transitions in ministry. She was there in good times and bad.

After a year of battling a prolapsed disk in her back, Myffie died in my arms at home on August 29, 1999. She lived to be eighteen and a half in human years and eighty-nine in dog years. She lived a good and long life. I miss her.

Myffie taught me what God's unconditional love is all about.

OBEDIENCE SCHOOL

In the summer of 1984, I enrolled my dog in obedience school. The classes were scheduled to last for six weeks. My objective for the course was to teach Myffie to become more obedient to my commands.

I took the course with her. We lasted only three weeks. As a result, I had to accept the fact that my dog was an obedience school dropout.

For her eighteen and a half years of life, Myffie was a good dog most of the time. She did have a stubborn streak that came out when I least expected it. She also got into some mischief at times (even in her later years). Oh, how I remember those days! However, she was a great canine companion that I loved and cared about. I miss her.

There are many people who are church dropouts. They leave the church for various reasons for which we don't understand. We miss them. We wonder what to say to those folks. Our first step could be by showing that we love and care for them.

Let's show our love for God and for the church dropouts
by reaching out.

SACRED PLACES

Almost ten years ago, I attended the Candler Christian Education Conference held at Emory University. While there, we learned a new term. It is called a sacred place. A sacred place is a place where one feels close to God and to one another. Every congregation has one. Every individual person can also have one.

I have several. I love the Georgia coast. I love the beach at Tybee Island. I love the piers at Epworth By the Sea on St. Simons Island. Even though I haven't been back there in years, I also love the grounds of my seminary campus at SMU in Dallas, Texas.

I really love sitting in my maternal grandfather's old rocking chair near the big window in my apartment. This is where I have my quiet time every morning. It is where I write in my journal, write down my prayer list, read and study the Scriptures and devotional materials, and pray.

At all these places, I feel a special closeness to God. It's like holy ground. At some of these places, I can see God's beautiful creation at hand. At all of these places, I can gain strength, wisdom, and love when I need it the most.

Do you have a sacred place?

39

GOD'S WAYS

In October 1988, my oldest sister, Joanne, and her husband, Bill, announced that they were expecting their second child the following April. In fact, the baby was due on April 11.

We were all excited about the news. Later that month, they found out that their baby would be a girl. They were thrilled because they already had a son. They decided to name their new daughter Jill.

In January 1989, I was over at Mom's house for dinner. I was in the kitchen looking at the calendar and discussing Jill's upcoming birth. While looking at the March 1989 calendar, I noticed that our grandmother (Mom's mother) would have turned one hundred years old (if she had lived that long) on March 17. A strange feeling came over me.

I said, "Mom, Joanne had her last baby (my nephew Philip) three weeks early. I have a feeling that she will give birth to Jill three weeks early. In fact, I believe that Jill will be born on the morning of March 17. But, please don't tell this to Joanne and Bill." She didn't.

I also shared this feeling with my coworkers at Cokesbury where I served on staff. On the week of March 12, they reminded me of that feeling. They asked me if I still felt the same way. I did.

At 6:30 A.M. on Friday, March 17, 1989, the telephone rang and woke me up. It was my mother. She said, "You were right!" I said, "Right about what?" She then said, "Jill was born this morning at 5:30. Mother and baby are doing fine. Jill was born on her great-grandmother's one hundredth birthday." I was stunned. I still am.

God works in mysterious ways.

40

HUSHPUPPIES

I t was a special evening at the 1991 North Georgia Annual Conference in Gainesville. I was asked to be the first diaconal minister to participate in the Annual Ordination Service. (My ordination as deacon in full connection was in 1997.) I was asked to serve as the Bible bearer for the service. It was an honor for diaconal ministry and also for me.

The processional began. It was beautiful and exciting. After the hymn was sung, I placed the Bible on the kneeling stand and headed toward my seat on stage near the ordinands. When we all sat down, I noticed how distinguished everyone looked in their clerical robes.

Most of the folks were wearing dark clothes to coordinate with their robes. All of the men were wearing nicely polished black leather shoes. I then looked at my feet. To my horror, I was still wearing my tan hushpuppies! Oh, how I wished that I had worn my black shoes.

I immediately tried to cover my shoes with my robe. That failed. I then tried to place them behind the plant near me. That also failed. I felt like a tan Pat Boone! I knew someone would notice. Some folks did. However, they said those shoes matched my personality. It was a soul-wrenching experience.

God's grace comes across through the loving souls of our Christian brothers and sisters.

MEMORABLE EASTER EGG HUNT

The Easter egg hunt at Harmony Grove UMC in Lilburn, Georgia, is always a big event each year. The egg hunt is always set up at Lanford Park, which is composed of two baseball fields and a picnic pavilion owned by the church. There are at least one hundred kids from the church and the Lilburn community that go to the Easter egg hunt there every year. The park is an ideal place to have the event.

During my tenure on staff at Harmony Grove, it was exciting to attend the Easter egg hunts. The weather was always beautiful. The kids and the adults had an absolute ball. For our 1996 Easter egg hunt, we again planned the event to be held at the Lanford Park. We also rented a moon walk for the kids to play on. It was planned to be a great event.

When I awoke the morning of the big event, I noticed that the skies were cloudy and dark. By the time I got to the church, it was raining. I didn't know if we should cancel the event or not. I prayed, "Lord, what are we going to do?" The children's coordinator got there and told me about a backup plan. I reluctantly agreed to it. We had an indoor Easter egg hunt in the church's gym. The moon walk was set up inside it and the kids went in to a room off the gym for their Easter egg hunt. We had over one hundred kids. They had a ball. It was still raining outside.

I had a teachable moment from that experience.

God does provide a Plan B.

42

RUNNING LATE

I woke up suddenly and looked at the clock. It was 6:30 A.M. I jumped out of bed thinking that I had overslept.

I don't like to run late. That's been a trait of mine since my childhood. I always like to be prompt and on time. Sometimes, I am too prompt. My family and friends used to kid me because I would show up fifteen minutes early at every event.

In fact, one day, I was scheduled to be at a supper group at 7:00 P.M. at a friend's house in Roswell. At 6:45, my friend's wife asked him, "Where's Don?" I was caught in traffic but arrived promptly at 7:00.

I just don't like to be late. Going back to that morning, I did oversleep. I got up and started to get ready for the day. I then realized something. As my sleepy eyes started to brighten up, I remembered that it was Thursday and my day off. I was already awake, so I started a load of laundry.

God calms our anxieties.

43

WEDDINGS

I enjoy weddings. Over the years, I had the honor of serving in several of them. I have served as an usher and groomsman in four weddings and as a best man in one. Since my ordination, I have officiated at several weddings which was, and still is, a true joy.

The first wedding that I officiated was for my youngest sister, Mary. Her wedding was scheduled for three days after I was ordained at annual conference. (This was my first ordination as deacon when I was in the process of elder's orders.) I co-officiated the wedding with a minister who was a family friend. It was wonderful.

Tears welled up in my eyes when Dad escorted Mary to the altar. I also got tearful when he escorted my sister Joanne to the altar a few years earlier. Come to the think of it, tears welled up when my brothers and my friends got married. Okay, I do cry at weddings. It marks a beginning of a whole new life. It's a joyous and a holy occasion.

To my dismay, some focus on the wedding with all its pageantry. After the wedding comes a marriage. Some folks put the emphasis on the wedding instead of on the marriage. Later, there can be trouble.

When a friend of mine got married ten years ago, she wanted a simple wedding and a fantastic marriage. She got her wish and had a simple but beautiful wedding. Her focus was on her marriage. It's a Christian commitment. Our walk with Christ can be viewed the same way. It's a committed relationship.

We all need to focus on our commitments to God.

44

EXERCISING

In May 2000, I bought a new compact exercise machine called the Ab Slide. The machine is supposed to be used to strengthen the abdominal muscles.

I have hopefully gained some wisdom as I have aged. I know that my weight has changed. For men after age thirty, everything seems to slide down. I have learned that my waist size can change very quickly. My dad taught me that after age forty we are on maintenance. Our bodies change and we need to take care of them.

So, I bought the Ab Slide machine to help in my exercise program. I have no plans to become Donald Schwarzenegger. I just want to tone up this middle-aged body. After talking with my doctor, I now work out with my Ab Slide five mornings a week. I also walk two miles three days a week.

Many of us know how to take care of ourselves physically. However, we also need to take care of ourselves spiritually.

God does not want our faith to slide.

45

SECURITY ALARMS

A t 6:00 A.M. on Sunday, July 23, 2000, I got up to get ready for the day. Around 6:10, I opened the front door of my apartment to get the morning paper and then went into the kitchen to make breakfast. As I was preparing the meal, I heard the beeping sound of the alarm system for my building.

The battery on the system was low and it beeps in every apartment until it is changed. There is a button that the residents can push to turn the beeping off. I went over to the alarm pad to turn off that button. My eyes were still sleepy at the time. As a result, I accidentally pushed the wrong button. I pushed the alarm button.

At 6:15, a loud alarm went off in my apartment. It had horns and sirens that could probably be heard throughout my side of the building. I tried to turn it off but I didn't know the code. I tried to call the alarm company but the alarm temporarily deadened the phone line. All that I was thinking was that my neighbors were going to love this. I was so embarrassed. Finally, the alarm went off after five minutes. I sat down and thanked God that it was over.

I went back into the kitchen to finish making my breakfast. Then it hit me. No one came knocking on my door to check to see if everything was okay. My alarm has never gone off before. I then started to think about what I should do if the alarm goes off in my neighbor's apartment. What would God want me to do? What would He want all of us to do?

God wants us to be good neighbors
and check on each other.

46

Making Time

During the year 2000, I had the opportunity to go on two trips to Tybee Island, Georgia. I took my first trip during my vacation in July. I took my second trip during my vacation in November. I love to walk the beach when I am down at the ocean. It's neat to get up and take an early morning walk. It's so peaceful, yet also rejuvenating to hear the roaring of the waves and the sounds of the seagulls.

The condo complex where I stayed is located on Tybee Bay. The bay beach is small but one can walk on it for about one and a half miles to get to the main beach. The waters are quiet and calm on the bay side. As you get closer to the main beach, the waves can be heard.

In July, I was able to take my early morning beach walks several times. They were so refreshing. I had some good talks with God during those walks. When I was down there in November, I got up early to have my morning walk on the beach. I went out on the pier and looked out at the bay. To my surprise, there was no beach. It was high tide.

I forgot about the change of seasons. The tides come in at a different time in November than they do in July. I got to have my beach walk, but it was in the afternoon.

It does not matter when each of us has a time with God. We each are on different schedules. Some of us function better at different times of the day than others.

It is important that we make time for God every day.

DAD'S ROLE MODEL

On May 1, 2001, DeKalb Medical Center in Decatur, Georgia, celebrated its fortieth birthday. It began as DeKalb General Hospital. My dad, William H. Thrasher, was the founding administrator and its first employee.

Dad was well loved by the hospital staff. He had a special gift with people. He would be seen walking around the hospital, checking to see how the staff members were doing. If someone was frustrated and had a concern, he would welcome that person into his office to talk about it. That person would leave the office smiling and feeling better about the situation.

Dad was known for his keen sense of humor. At the 1961 open house when the hospital was dedicated, there were many people still in the building touring the hospital. Several doctors and nurses were concerned about having time to get ready for the opening day the next morning. Dad got on the public announcement system and announced, "Visiting hours are now over."

Over the eighteen years since his death, I have grown to appreciate my dad even more. Even though he was human, he acted the same at home as he did at the office. Even in his illness, Dad was caring, loving, cheerful, humorous, wise, and served as a peacemaker. He was a genuine Christian who taught through his faith and life. His role model was Jesus Christ.

Jesus is a powerful role model for all of us.

48

QUIET TIME

I enjoy talking with friends and relatives. It is always good to touch base with them. Now with e-mail, I talk more though the computer with brief messages than I talk with folks on the phone. E-mail is easier and quicker at times. However, there is nothing like actually talking with someone.

There are folks that I talk with daily, a couple of times a week, weekly, or even monthly. Our conversations deal with how each is doing, what is going on in our lives, and even different problems that we each face.

Quiet time is a period set aside for each of us to have and develop a personal relationship with God. It is a time for study, Scripture reading and devotions, and a time for prayer. It is a time to tell God how we are doing, what is going on in our lives, and the different problems that we each face. It is also a time for listening.

With it, no phone cards or credit cards are needed. We each have a twenty-four-hour toll-free open line always available to us.

Quiet time is the way for each of us to touch base with God.

DREAMS

I have had many lifelong dreams. Some have come true and some have not. Sadly, some never will. Several dreams of mine have come true. I received a master's degree. I went to school at SMU. I owned a dog. I have been able to serve as a Christian educator on staff in a local church. I have traveled through parts of the United States. I have become an uncle six times and now have recently become a great-uncle. I have written and published the inspirational book you are reading right now.

There are those dreams that have not yet come true. I would like to buy a home (a retirement or vacation condo on Tybee Island). I would like to be married some day and maybe have a child (even in my late forties or early fifties).

There are also dreams that will not come true. I wanted my dad to serve as best man at my wedding. I wanted him to see my child—his grandchild. I wanted him to see me consecrated as a diaconal minister and later ordained as a deacon in full connection. Because of his death, none of these will happen. However, Dad was and will always be here in spirit.

All of us have dreams. Isn't it comforting to know that God is with us no matter if our dreams come true or not?

God's love is an everlasting dream.

LOOKING IN THE MIRROR

One day, I stopped by a drugstore on the way home from the office to pick up a few things. One item that I picked up was a hand mirror to help me when I put my contact lenses in. When I got home, I went into the bathroom to put the mirror in a drawer. I stopped for a moment and put the mirror behind my head. I looked into the bathroom mirror and saw the top of my head. (I had been putting off seeing it for years.)

I looked at it and saw a bald spot in my hair. I said. "Uh oh. I have to call Hair Club for Men!" I looked again. There I saw my dad's head and hairline. I thought, "If he could live with it, I can too." It's my heritage.

When was the last time that you really looked in the mirror? When you looked, did you remember the past? Did you reflect on all the times that God has shaped you? Did you realize your heritage?

It is now the time to take what we have reflected on and move on to what lies ahead. We need to continue to be the unique church that God called us to be. It is our heritage. It is also our future.

God will guide us every step of the way.

TRIP BACK TO TEXAS

I n April 2001, I had the wonderful opportunity to attend the Rivers of Faith, an adult ministries event in San Antonio, Texas. The training event was sponsored by the General Board of Discipleship of the United Methodist Church.

It was my first trip back to Texas in over nineteen years. My last time back was in 1982 for minister's week at SMU in Dallas. During my seminary years in Texas, I traveled to many of its cities. However, I had not been to San Antonio. I really looked forward to this trip.

When I arrived at the hotel where the event was held, the first people that I ran into were from Atlanta! Later, I had several reunions with friends with whom I went to seminary. Some I hadn't seen since graduation. It was so good to see those folks. It was fun to catch up with each other and our ministries. It was also interesting to catch up on the news of other classmates.

I had a reunion with one friend whom I had not seen in nearly twenty-three years. He was from San Antonio and showed me around the city. Glenn had dropped out of seminary because he felt another calling. We had a great reunion.

The training event was awesome. The workshops and the speakers were absolutely excellent. I am still processing all the information that I received. The Texas trip was surely a blessing.

God gives us moments to appreciate
where we come from, where we are,
and where we are going in our journeys of faith.

ABOUT THE AUTHOR

D on Thrasher is an ordained Christian Educator and Deacon in Full Connection in the North Georgia Conference of the United Methodist Church. He received his B.S. degree in psychology from Georgia College (now Georgia College and State University) and his Master of Theology degree from Southern Methodist University. He has spent most of his Christian education ministry serving on staff of neighborhood churches in metro Atlanta.